GIRLS GUIDES

Write It Down!

A Girl's Guide to Keeping a Journal

● Erica Smith ●

the rosen publishing group's
rosen central
new york

In memory of my mother, Deborah Shoemaker Smith, for the diaries she kept.

In memory of Anaïs Nin (1903–1977). *I know that human beings place upon an object, or a person, the responsibility of being the obstacle when the obstacle always lies within one's self.*

In memory of Anne Frank (1929–1945). *Thank you, God, for all that is good and dear and beautiful.*

Published in 1999 by The Rosen Publishing Group, Inc.
29 East 21st Street, New York, NY 10010

First Edition

Library of Congress Cataloging-in-Publication Data

Smith, Erica.
     Write it down! a girl's guide to keeping a journal / Erica
Smith. — 1st ed.
       p.   cm. — (Girls' guides)
     Includes bibliographical references (p. 45) and index.
     Summary: Discusses journal writing as a useful and fun activity to
help girls learn about themselves and express their thoughts and
feelings.
     ISBN 0-8239-2979-5
     1. Diaries—Authorship Juvenile literature. 2. Girls—Diaries—Authorship
Juvenile literature.   [1. Diaries.]   I. Title. II. Series.
PN4390.S64   1999
808'.06692—dc21   99-20117
                                           CIP

Manufactured in the United States of America

Contents

bout This Book

The middle school years are like a roller coaster—wild and scary but also fun and way cool. One minute you're way, way up there, and the next minute you're plunging down into the depths. Not surprisingly, sometimes you may find yourself feeling confused and lost. Not to worry, though. Just like on a roller-coaster ride, at the end of all this crazy middle school stuff, you'll be laughing and screaming and talking about how awesome it all was.

Right now, however, chances are your body is changing so much that it's barely recognizable, your old friends may not share your interests anymore, and your life at school is suddenly hugely complicated. And let's not even get into the whole boy issue. It's a wonder that you can still think straight at all.

Fortunately, reader dear, help is here. This book is your road map. It's also a treasure chest filled with ideas and advice. Armed with this book and with your own inner strength (trust us, you have plenty), you can safely, confidently navigate the twists and turns of your middle school years. It will be tough going, and sometimes you'll wonder if you'll ever get through it. But you—fabulous, powerful, unique you—are up to the task. This book is just a place to start.

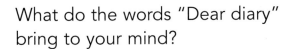

Dear Diary. . .

What do the words "Dear diary" bring to your mind?

 A brave Anne Frank hiding out with her family as the Nazis took over Amsterdam during World War II, writing the diary that later would take a place in history?

A desperate teenage Winona Ryder scrawling wildly across journal pages, all alone in her room in the movie **Heathers**, because she hates her friends?

 Your English teacher requiring you to keep a journal about your deepest, most intimate thoughts regarding the recurring image of the chimney in the novels of Charles Dickens?

Okay, so (almost) all of the above are (kind of) real-life examples of keeping a journal. But the world of journal writing is a big one.

If you're really desperate to write about Charles Dickens and his chimneys, go right ahead. But in this book, we're going to talk about you.

Hello? So What Is "Journal Writing," Anyway?

Diary keeping, journal writing, or journaling, they all mean the same thing: recording your thoughts.

Yes, thoughts. We know you have them. Sometimes you broadcast them to everyone within earshot. Other times you seal them inside of yourself quite tightly. (Don't think no one noticed.)

But what if you feel like broadcasting your thoughts—and no one's around? Or what if you're holding in your feelings so tightly that you'll explode if you don't get them out somehow?

That's where a journal comes in.

Writing down your thoughts in a little "blank book" is an excellent way to make sense of everything that's going on inside (and outside) of you. It's like having a secret best friend you can tell everything to—someone who listens and doesn't pass judgment. And unlike your real best friend, whose parents may not appreciate 2 AM phone calls, a journal is at your fingertips 24-7.

Yes, but I Hate to Write

Easy there, tiger. "Hate" is a very strong word.

Perhaps you're really trying to say that you're just a tiny bit worried. You've never been crowned School Grammar Queen. You are not Shakespeare-in-Training when it comes to writing stories in class. What if you start to write stuff down and it sounds really dumb and embarrassing?

Lay your worries aside, sister. They don't matter now.

Think for a minute about what it means to keep a journal. Has it dawned on you that you will be the only one reading it? So even if spelling errors are littered across the page, your handwriting comes out as wonky as Jewel's crooked tooth, and you write about pigs flying over the moon, no one is going to know.

Besides, isn't it beautiful not to be so-called perfect? Spelling is an art, not a science. Jewel refused to have that tooth straightened—and you can see how much it's hurt her record sales. And if pigs ever do fly over the moon, you'll be right there to record it.

Get Serious

Now that you have laid to rest all the butterflies in your stomach, there's one more reason why keeping a journal is so cool. For girls especially, keeping a journal is a handy way to keep your brain sane as you catapult into the crazy teen years. And after the whirlwind is over, you can look back at your journals and—yes, scream in embarrass- ment—but also see how much you've learned.

For some girls, keep- ing a journal is a way of life, lasting far into adulthood. It can help you get through tough situations when you're an adult, just as it does

Cool Quotes

Life shrinks or expands in proportion to one's courage.
—Anaïs Nin, writer, famous for her lifelong diary

when you're a teen. The situations may be different, but your journal will be just the same: a place to confide your thoughts, hopes, and fears without worrying about being judged or criticized.

Your journal can help you make sense of the world when the world isn't making any sense to you. It will listen to you when it seems as if no one else will. It can even bring you closer to your life's dreams.

So stay tuned—and hang on!

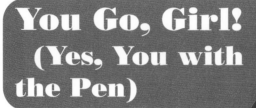

2

You Go, Girl! (Yes, You with the Pen)

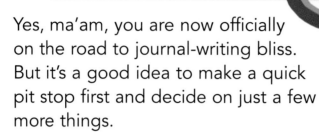

Yes, ma'am, you are now officially on the road to journal-writing bliss. But it's a good idea to make a quick pit stop first and decide on just a few more things.

Gettin' the Goods

For one thing, journal writing requires you to gather some simple tools. But before you buy, consider the following details. You want your book to be:

Affordable

How much money do you have to spend? You can spend as little as $1.99 for a notebook at the drugstore, or you can dish out between $5 and $10—or more—for a blank book with a decorative cover like the ones on display at your local bookstore.

Yes, you want to get something fun. But you don't want to have to baby-sit every night of your life in order to keep up your wild journaling habit. Our advice: Keep it simple. There are many ways to jazz up even a plain spiral notebook. (Read on, and you'll find out how.)

Portable

Do you want to have your journal handy when you're bored stiff in study hall? Get a lightweight book that will fit comfortably in your knapsack. Plan on writing only in bed? Go ahead and get a book the size of *Moby Dick.*

Private

You probably don't want anyone snooping around your precious book. Consider a safe place to keep your journal. If you're really concerned, think about a lock and key (more on this later).

Yours

This may sound obvious, but remember: Your little diary is yours and yours alone. So get whatever you want! It's your style and attitude that make your diary (and you!) truly fabulous.

Jump start

It's never too early to start thinking about what you're going to write. Try these ideas:
- *Describe five great things about yourself.*
- *What is one memory you have from first grade?*

Exterior Decorating

There are many things you can do to spice up your journal. If you're feeling crafty, check out your local fabric store. You can find an

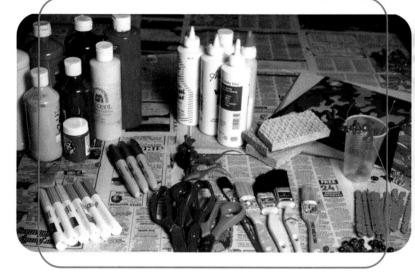

inexpensive journal-size scrap of cloth—even velvet—that would look mighty fine on the cover of your book. You can lay it down using simple fabric glue.

You can also create designs using ribbon, rubber stamps, buttons, pebbles, jingle bell balls, tiny plastic dinosaurs . . . you get the idea.

Psst!

Hint

If you're using fabric, put glue on the underside corners of the journal cover and fold the fabric over the corners to make it stick. That should be enough to hold it. Don't spread glue all over the cover, because then everything will get messy-wet.

Think twice about using glitter, though—especially if you're carrying your journal around with you. You're bound to have a KGE (Knapsack Glitter Explosion). Not cool!

If you're supercreative, you can even make your own paper or bind store-bought paper into a book. Try looking for a paper-making kit in a craft store, see if a local college or book arts center offers classes in bookmaking, or check out the resources listed in It's a Girl's World, at the end of this book.

Make sure that before you start any craft project—no matter how small—you follow these all-important steps:

#1 Tell an adult what you're doing, and find a work space that is acceptable to you AND the adult(s) in your home.

#2 Cover the work space with newspaper while you're working.

#3 Wear old, sloppy clothes in case of spills, splatters, or other mishaps.

#4 Put on your favorite CD to help you get in a creative mood. (But be careful not to dance so wildly that you knock your supplies off the table.)

#5 Have an adult with you when you use potentially harmful materials such as rubber cement or other funky glues. Read the labels of all craft materials before you use them.

#6 Clean your work area, your tools (scissors, paintbrushes, etc.), and yourself afterward.

It's a girl's world; it pays to be smart!

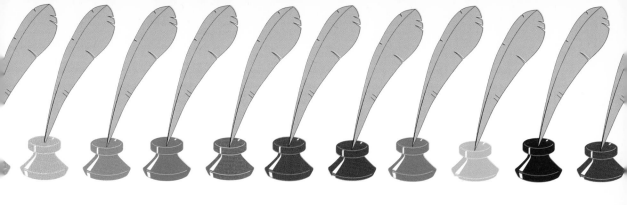

A Word on Writing Implements

"A pen is just a pen," you say. Think again.

Mmmm, yes . . . as with kisses, there are pens and then there are pens. There are ballpoint pens, felt tip pens, rolling-ball pens, ten-barreled multicolor pens, pens of fine point or extrafine point, clicky pens, and erasable pens. Let's not even get into pencils!

The point (get it?) is, for about $1.50 at any stationery store, you can probably find a groovy little writing implement that is waiting just for you. Pick a color that you like.

Virtual Journals

If you're a high-tech kind of gal, you may find it easier to put your deep thoughts on the computer instead of in a book. That works too, of course. Just remember that if you share a computer, you'll need to create your journal in a program that allows you to protect individual files with a password. (Most word processing

programs will let you do this.) Otherwise, everyone who sits down at the computer—your parents, your siblings, even your bratty little cousin who likes to play computer games whenever she visits—will be able to read what you've written. And you don't want that to happen, do you?

Another thing to remember about on-line journaling is that the computer allows you to rewrite and correct what you've written much more easily than you can with pen and paper. That can be a good thing because it allows you to say exactly what you want to say, exactly the way you want to say it. But you also may find that it encourages you to edit your feelings and to rewrite stuff you wrote when you were angry or sad that you now regret. Pen and paper make your journal more spontaneous and maybe just a bit more real. But if you're happier pouring your heart out onto the keyboard instead of into a book, a computer journal is the way to go.

Whichever you choose, congratulations: You have now found your special writing tool, the magic wand that will help you on your journal-writing journey.

Onward!

3

Let's Get Writing!

Look around. There's so much going on. For one thing, you're in a totally new place in life. You're on the brink of your teens—the wackiest years you will ever experience.

Aren't you glad you have a journal with you to help you through it?

Yes, indeed—by this very moment you should have a journal and a writing implement by your side. (If you don't, reread chapter two and act accordingly.) So now it's time to get cracking. This chapter will give you some ideas as you sit down and start to write.

Tune In

One of the first things you can do is mark your journal as truly your own. List:

Your name
Your address
Start date
Your age

Be sure to leave a space at the end of the journal for your vital stats when you've completed your book.

dating rules

Your first entry, like all of your entries, can be about whatever you want: a simple chronicle

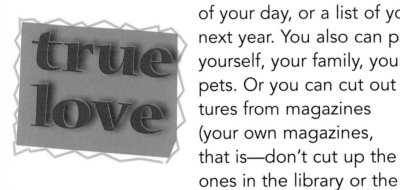

true love

of your day, or a list of your goals for the next year. You also can paste in pictures of yourself, your family, your friends, and your pets. Or you can cut out words and pictures from magazines (your own magazines, that is—don't cut up the ones in the library or the dentist's office, please!) and use them to create a cool collage about yourself.

sister power

Jump start

Describe a typical school day.
  • *Who is your best friend? What do you talk about when you're together?*

Dream a Little Dream

Chances are, you have some big ideas about what you want out of life. Good! Write them down. Where do you want to be when you're eighteen, twenty-five, even thirty?

Describe a typical day you envision for yourself fifteen years from now. Are you headlining with your band on the Lilith Fair tour? Are you a photographer for the *New York Times*, stationed in Beijing? Are you hard at work in a laboratory, finding a cure for cancer? Are you preparing to go to law school?

These goals may seem a

what do I want to be?

If one is lucky, a solitary fantasy can totally transform one million realities.
—Maya Angelou,
writer and entertainer

long way off, but they're not. Pick up that guitar/camera/microscope/law encyclopedia now! And write in your journal about the progress you make toward achieving your dreams.

People Who Need People

When you're not busy imagining how you're going to save the world, you can write about people who are right next to you. Let's start with the family.

Maybe there's a great story your aunt told you—you know, the one about the time she accidentally put the car in reverse while leaning over to give a big good-bye smooch to her date, and the car ended up rolling into a cornfield—that could be immortalized in your little diary. That way, you'll never forget it (even if your aunt was kind of hoping you would)!

Also, if you have grandparents or other older people in your life, you can write about them and keep track of some of the stories they tell. Many teens feel awkward around their parents and grandparents. But writing about them may help ease that feeling. At the same time, by keeping in touch with the older generations, you'll be helping to build your family history.

You also can use your journal to think about spending

Jump start

- *Pick a person in your family and describe your feelings for him or her. How did you view this person when you were little? How do you view him or her now?*
- *If you could be any animal, what would you be? Why?*

time with new people. Is there someone you really look up to—your sister, a cousin, your former baby-sitter? Write down some ideas for hanging out with this person. Then call her up and make plans!

All You Need Is Love

Ah, yes. Love, love, love is on your mind. For the pages and pages you may devote to writing about your crush's lilting voice and heart-melting eyes, for the endless doodling of that special name . . . your journal is right by your side.

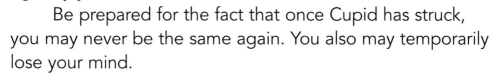

Be prepared for the fact that once Cupid has struck, you may never be the same again. You also may temporarily lose your mind.

"Cool Quotes"

Love's sweet bells are ringing again!
—from the author's diary, age thirteen. (Ugh.)

You've Got to Have Friends

No matter how inspiring all of your romantic daydreams are, don't forget your best buds. Rumor has it you do some pretty crazy stuff together. Well, here's one more thing to try! Start journals at the same time. Then when you're hanging out, you can write together.

"Cool Quotes"

The giving of love is an education in itself.
—Eleanor Roosevelt, American stateswoman and humanitarian

Take a Jump Start and write separate responses to it. Then share what you came up with. This can be tons more fun than dishing out your allowance to see the latest flick at the multiplex or milling around the mall.

Jump start

- Write *about a special day you spent together with your bud.*
- *If you could take a trip anywhere with your friends, where would you go? Why?*

Keep Out!

NO TRESPASSING

4

On any list of things that are important to you, privacy is probably right at the top. This is true for most girls. It means privacy for your body (proof: the locker room clothes-changing maneuver, or the Shim Sham Slip-on Dance, as *Mode* magazine calls it) and also your mind—your deepest, most confidential feelings.

Part of keeping a journal is being able to express these innermost feelings so that they don't stay bottled up inside of you. And let's face it—some of what you have to say is less than polite.

You may write a long, ranting diary entry because your mom asked you to do your homework just one too many times. Or you're annoyed with your brother for putting his pet iguana under your pillow, and you write a long passage comparing him (unfavorably) to Godzilla.

This is fine. This is normal.

But no matter what you say in your journal, chances are you want to keep it to yourself—at least for now. That's why it's useful to learn some snoop-proofing maneuvers.

COOL QUOTES

Mama may have,
Papa may have,
But God bless the child
That's got his own.
—Billie Holiday,
"God Bless the Child"

Snooping Is Uncool, Charlie Brown

The first rule is to gently let people know that this is your journal and it's private.

Ma and Pa may have noticed that one bright day, you brought home a notebook, pens, glue, and ribbons and whipped them all up into a mysterious, funky-looking book. They may have noticed that you sit with your face buried in this funky-looking book for hours on end, your nose scrunched up like a little mousie nibbling on cheese, and scrawl precious words. They may have noticed the glitter trail flowing from your knapsack (because you ignored the warning about the KGE, didn't you?).

Face it. They're worried. You've been acting strange enough already. And now this?

To nip this problem in the bud, take a minute and tell them

what you're doing. Say, "I've read this fabulous book about journal writing, and I'm trying it for myself. Please respect my privacy and don't read my journal." For most parents, that statement works wonders as a simple, respectful way to draw the line.

The same goes for siblings, too—even the young'uns. Amazingly, most people are pretty reasonable if you ask them in a clear, serious, and straightforward way.

At all costs, avoid using Lucy Van Pelt's Five Good Reasons. ("One . . . two . . . three . . . four . . . five!" she counts off, clenching her fingers into a menacing fist and shaking it in Linus's face when he asks her for one good reason why he should listen to her.) When you use threats and force, you are almost daring someone to raid your diary and prance around the house chanting the name of your latest crush.

Jump start

- *Describe a time when someone was really there for you. What did this person say or do that helped you?*
- *Describe a time when you were disappointed by a person. Did you express your disappointment? If not, how would you do it now?*

Park It

Now that you've had your heart-to-heart with the family, you should be able to leave your journal wherever you want—on your nightstand or with your schoolbooks—and not worry about it.

But if you're still feeling queasy about the possibility of being snooped upon, think about a strategic location to keep your journal. ("Hide" sounds a bit extreme, doesn't it?)

Go all out. Mush the book under your mattress. Place it in

your panty drawer. Cloak it in your closet. Wedge it in the windowsill. Bury it in the cat box.

Okay, maybe not the cat box. But you get the point.

When Your Worst Fear Has Come True

You hear a song drifting through the air. It's faint, but it's getting closer, louder. It's the voice of your little brother. Suddenly he's standing in your doorway, iguana in one hand, your journal (wide open) in the other. He's singing the name of your crush . . . over and over and over.

Or . . .

You're watching television with Mom. It's a commercial—one with a mother and daughter having a heartfelt conversation about feminine products.

Your mom turns to you. With tears welling up in her eyes, she blurts out, "Honey, I'm so sorry I didn't stick up for you when the doctor was surprised that you didn't have your period yet. I know his comment hurt you."

Oh no.

Oh no, no, no.

You've been snooped.

If this really does happen to you—if someone confronts you with a bit of information that only your diary should know—you may react in several ways. The most obvious is with anger, which is normal. You feel betrayed and invaded.

There's another side to the story, though. After your reaction of shock and anger, you need to sit down with the snooper and have yet another heart-to-heart. You must ask again that your diary stay off-limits. You also must ask why this person peeked.

It's possible, especially with a parent, that he or she peeked as a desperate way to try to find out who, exactly, you are. Remember, it wasn't too long ago that your parents were diapering your little tushie and picking out your clothes for you. And suddenly you've turned into a mutant! . . . oops, er . . . you've blossomed into a teenager. You're a brand-new person, and your folks are probably baffled.

Take pity on your poor snoopers and forgive them. There may be a few bumps along the way, but if you try, you can build trust with people, share feelings, and still have your privacy.

Stop, Drop, and Think

5

Speaking of privacy, let's take a quick detour.

Do any of these diary entries sound like they could come from you?

Today I ate only half a slice of toast for breakfast, two oranges for lunch, and a diet cola for dinner. But, ugh! I feel so fat! My stomach hurts. I wonder how many calories there are in gum.

I feel so blue I can hardly get out of bed in the morning. I feel like crying all the time. I don't know what to do about this. Nobody would believe me if I told them. Besides, how can I ask for help when I don't even know what's wrong?

I wish I hadn't tried drugs with D.J. I know it's wrong, but he treated me with so much more respect after I got high with him. He wants me to do it again, but I'm not sure.

As you know, a journal is a great place to confide your fears, hurts, and mistakes. But if something is going on in your life that feels dangerous or over-whelming, it's time to tell some-one other than your diary.

Many teens find themselves in situations such as these:

 You are constantly worried about becoming overweight, and you either strictly limit how much you eat or overeat in "binges" (or both).

Verbal abuse or physical violence is taking place in your family.

 You are involved with someone in a sexual way, whether or not you want to be.

 You are being pressured to try drugs, or you already are using them.

 You are having overwhelming feelings of sadness that interfere with your daily life.

You may be deeply troubled by one of these situations or by something else, and you might feel as if there is no one to talk to. But there is.

Tell someone that you need help. Even with your diary at your side, certain situations put your safety in danger. They are too big to handle alone.

Although it may feel awkward at first, you should talk immediately to an adult you trust. Ask your parents, a friend's parents, a teacher, a guidance counselor, a coach, or someone from your religious group if you can have a few minutes of their time. Tell them what is wrong. They can listen to you and help you decide what to do. You also can call one of the hotlines listed at the back of this book.

The same is true if it's a friend of yours who is in a situation that she can't handle. She may be confiding in you and even asking you for help. Lend her a shoulder when she needs one, confide in your diary that you're worried about her—but don't think that you can handle or solve her problems on your own. Offer to help her find a counselor or other adult to talk to.

Thanks for listening, and please take action if you need to.

Writing, Reading, and Rereading

6

Have you ever woken up slowly, pulling out of a dream that seemed almost too exquisite for words? And then as soon as your eyes were open, the details of your dream—the source of your bliss—completely evaporated from your brain, never to be heard from again?

Frustrating, huh?

Now think of your daytime thoughts. Yes, your wittiest, most excellent observations come to mind. But also think of what happens every day: conversations with friends, funny stuff that happens at school.

Some memories stay with you for a long time. But a year from now, do you really think you'll remember all the words to the song you made up about your crazy history teacher?

Well, keeping a journal means that you're creating a place to house all of these goings-on. Unlike your brain, a journal doesn't forget. As your journal is slowly filled with your precious words, you're making sure that the details of your life don't just fly out on the wind. Like the Greek gods and goddesses high on Olympus, you are becoming—in your own small way—immortal.

If you've started your journal already, pick it up and read. You're looking into the past, which can be thrilling.

And mortifying, of course.

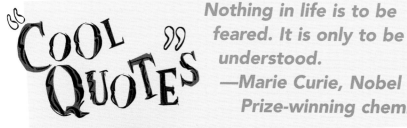

"COOL QUOTES"

Nothing in life is to be feared. It is only to be understood.
—Marie Curie, Nobel Prize-winning chemist

I Can't Believe I Said That!

You're turning beet red because you're reading a passage you wrote in your journal declaring your undying love for a certain somebody. But in reality your love went *poof* three weeks ago, you've had two better crushes since then, and frankly, you'd like to forget that you ever laid eyes on the person in question.

You have the impulse to tear the offending page out of your journal and stomp on it until the pulpy paper disintegrates into the ground. Stomp, stomp, stomp!

Okay, now, take it easy. Relax.

Yes, journals immortalize some of your most misguided thoughts. But you can use them as a learning experience. Instead of cursing the ink on your old journal pages, try to read with a clear eye and an open heart. Forgive yourself for the silly things you may have done in the past. There are so many more silly things to get started on for your future!

Jump start

- *Try keeping a journal and pen at your bedside. Next time you have an excellent, vivid dream, write down everything you can remember as soon as you wake up. Then write down what you think it means. Six months later, go back and reread your dream notes. What do you think of them now?*

The Moral of the Story

If you get into the habit of reading what you've written every six months or so, you'll start to gain some clarity about who you are and where you're going. Sometimes you'll get hit in the head—thunk!—with a realization that you never would have had otherwise.

Congratulations on your new self-knowledge!

Jump start

- *How are you similar to each of your parents? How are you different?*
- *When was the last time you tried something new? What was it? How did it go? Would you do it again?*

As you set out on your journey to self-awareness, try asking yourself questions like these or any of a zillion others that you might think of.

Carry It On

7

Now that you have started your journal, who knows the places you'll go?

Through the years, through all of the craziness that is sure to come, your journal will help you keep your feet on the ground.

Someone to Watch Over Me

As your journal is gradually filled with even more gems from your soul, you may decide that there are new avenues to explore.

For one, you might decide that it's time to loosen the reins on the privacy business.

Have a friend or family member write in your journal, or even read parts of it out loud together. Friends are for sharing, right?

Also, try taking a passage from your journal and rewriting it, filling it out a little here and there. A true-life story can blossom into a great short story or even a novel!

If you'd rather be a rock star than a best-selling novelist, remember that many songwriters use their journals as a place to sketch out words and ideas for their songs. If you're still shooting for the Lilith tour, start here!

You also can use sketch pads as a way to combine your artistic and literary talents. Get out your markers or your watercolors and illustrate the events of your day or the secrets of your heart as well as writing about them. Or try making a journal entry using only pictures, without any words.

What if you're not feeling all that creative? No problem. Just jot down whatever is in your head on any topic. Maybe you'll be inspired the next time you write, and maybe not. The only limits on what can go into your journal are the ones that you set yourself.

Ev'ry Time We Say Good-bye

Alas, we have come to the end of our magic carpet ride through the magical world of journals.

But I know your heart will go on. At the end of this book, you'll find other places and sources that can help you hook up to new people, new ideas. Don't be shy! Call up and see what's cooking. It's a girl's world, and it's time to get

in on the action! By now you've probably thought of count-
less ideas for what your journal will look like and what you'll
put in it. So pick up your pen and start writing.

Take heart, sisters, and keep in touch.

It's a Girl's World:
helpful info

Paper and Bookmaking Stuff

Pearl Art and Crafts
579 Massachusetts Avenue
Cambridge, MA 02139
(617) 547-6600

Rugg Road Papers
105 Charles Street
Boston, MA 02114
(617) 742-0002

Girl Stuff

Big Brothers Big Sisters of America
230 North 13th Street
Philadelphia, PA 19107
(215) 567-7000
Web site: http://www.bbsa.org.
A cool place to meet an older girl that you can spend
    time with and learn from!

Girls Incorporated
120 Wall Street, 3rd Floor
New York, NY 10005
(212) 509-2000
Web site: http://www.girlsinc.org

Through informal education, this organization helps
   encourage girls to reach for their dreams.

Youth Crisis Hotline
(800) 448-4663; (800) 999-9999

YWCA of the USA
Empire State Building, Suite 301
350 Fifth Avenue
New York, NY 10118
(212) 273-7800
Web site: http: www.ywca.org
Offers programs in physical fitness, first aid, education,
   and leadership.

On-line Stuff
Girl Power!
http://www.health.org/gpower/girlarea

Girl Zone
http://www.girlzone.com

gURL online magazine
http://www.gurl.com

New Moon: The Magazine for Girls and Their Dreams
http://www.newmoon.org

By the Book: *further reading*

Aldrich, Anne H. *Notes from Myself: A Guide to Creative Journal Writing.* New York: Carroll & Graf Publishers, Inc., 1998.

Frank, Anne. *The Diary of a Young Girl: The Definitive Edition.* Ed. Otto H. Frank and Mirjam Pressler. New York: Anchor Books, 1995.

Gutkind, Lee. *Creative Nonfiction: How to Live It and Write It.* Chicago: Ziggurat Books, 1996.

Hopper, Nancy J. *Jazmin's Notebook.* New York: Dial Books, 1998.

Hunter, Latoya. *The Diary of Latoya Hunter: My First Year in Junior High.* New York: Random House, Inc., 1993.

Lyons, Mary E. *Keeping Secrets: The Girlhood Diaries of Seven Women Writers.* New York: Henry Holt & Co., Inc., 1995.

McCarthy, Mary, and Philip Manna. *Making Books by Hand: A Step-by-Step Guide.* Gloucester, MA: Quarry Books, 1997.

Stevens, Carla. *A Book of Your Own: Keeping a Diary or Journal.* New York: Clarion Books, 1993.

Weston, Carol. *For Girls Only: Wise Words, Good Advice.* New York: Avon Books, 1998.

Wilber, Jessica. *Totally Private and Personal: Journaling Ideas for Girls and Young Women.* Minneapolis, MN: Free Spirit Publishing, Inc., 1996.

Woodward, Patricia. *Journal Jumpstarts: Quick Topics and Tips for Journal Writing.* Fort Collins, CO: Cottonwood Press, Inc., 1991.

Index

Credits

Acknowledgments
A loud thank-you meow to Amy Haugesag, editor at the Rosen Publishing Group, for your deep love of books, cats, and trash. Thank-you to Laura Murawski for your stunning design and unflappable spirit, and to Gertie the Girl Guide for your exquisite blue beauty.

About the Author
Erica Smith lives in Brooklyn, New York, where she writes a lot and sings even more. She has been keeping journals since the age of eight and shows no signs of stopping. She is the author of *Anorexia Nervosa: When Food Is the Enemy*, also published by Rosen.

Photo Credits
Cover photo by Thaddeus Harden; pp.12, 14, 40–41 by Christine Innamorato; p. 17 by Pablo Maldonado; p. 31 by Maike Schultz; p. 33 by John Nova; p.34 © Archive Photos; all other photos by Thaddeus Harden.

Design and Layout
Laura Murawski

DATE DUE

FE 11 '08			

#47-0108 Peel Off Pressure Sensitive